<h1 style="text-align:center">MALDIVES 2016 HUMAN RIGHTS REPORT</h1>

EXECUTIVE SUMMARY

The Republic of Maldives is a multiparty constitutional democracy. Abdulla Yameen Abdul Gayoom won the presidential election in 2013 in what most international observers and local nongovernmental organization (NGO) Transparency Maldives (TM) determined to be a credible and transparent election. Parliamentary elections held in March 2014 were also well administered and transparent, according to TM, although there were reports of vote buying due to shortcomings in the legal system and lack of enforcement.

Civilian authorities maintained effective control over the security forces.

The most significant human rights problems included efforts by parliament, courts, and police to restrict freedoms of speech and assembly; reports of a politicized and inefficient judiciary; and reports of corruption of senior government officials.

Other human rights problems included the use of flogging as a punishment, detention of political prisoners, restrictions on religious freedom, targeted harassment and arbitrary detention of journalists, abuse and unequal treatment of women, employment discrimination on the basis of political opinion, and discrimination against foreign laborers. Migrant laborers experienced labor abuses and were the primary victims of human trafficking. In August parliament passed an antidefamation law that the UN special rapporteur on freedom of expression asserted limited the right to freedom of expression to such a degree that the right itself was in jeopardy.

The government did not take steps to prosecute and punish police and military officers who committed abuses.

Section 1. Respect for the Integrity of the Person, Including Freedom from:

a. Arbitrary Deprivation of Life and other Unlawful or Politically Motivated Killings

There were no reports that the government or its agents committed arbitrary or unlawful killings.

b. Disappearance

There were no reports of politically motivated disappearances.

In April Chief Inspector of Police Abdulla Satheeth publicly stated unknown persons had abducted *Minivan News* (now *Maldives Independent*) journalist and human rights advocate Ahmed Rilwan Abdulla, the first acknowledgement from police of foul play in Rilwan's 2014 disappearance. A delegation from the government traveled to Geneva in May to provide information on the investigation into Rilwan's disappearance to the UN Working Group on Enforced and Involuntary Disappearances, but the United Nations had not published its findings by year's end. In July police released the only two suspects held in connection with Rilwan's disappearance, citing a lack of evidence linking them to the incident. As of August law enforcement's working hypothesis was that members of an organized gang abducted Rilwan because of his criticisms of gang violence and Islamic radicalization. Rilwan's family, however, continued to blame publicly senior government officials for his disappearance and accused police of negligence in the handling of the case. The National Integrity Commission (NIC) continued to investigate the allegations against police but reported its preliminary assessment that police were timely in response to reports of Rilwan's disappearance.

c. Torture and Other Cruel, Inhuman, or Degrading Treatment or Punishment

The constitution prohibits such practices, but the law permits flogging and other forms of corporal punishment, and security officials employed such practices.

The Prosecutor General's Office (PGO) reported it received and prosecuted one case of torture and other cruel, inhuman, or degrading treatment or punishment during the year, but it did not disclose the identities of the defendant or plaintiff. According to the Human Rights Commission of Maldives' (HRCM) third annual antitorture report released in 2016, the Maldives Police Service (MPS) was accused in 48 of the 55 cases of torture submitted to them between July 2015 and June 2016. The victims were under the age of 18 in three of the cases alleging police torture. The HRCM completed investigations in 46 of the 55 cases and found no evidence of torture in any cases. There were several allegations of police brutality from journalists and opposition protesters who were routinely arrested during antigovernment protests.

A regulation permits flogging as a form of punishment. As of September the courts sentenced six women and three men to flogging. According to an October

2014 Supreme Court guideline, the court must delay the execution of a flogging sentence on minors until they reach the age of 18. The Penal Code, which came into effect in July 2015, does not provide for banishment as a sentence, and there were no new banishment sentences during the year. The Maldives Correctional Service (MCS), however, reported there were nine persons still serving their banishment sentences.

Prison and Detention Center Conditions

Although overcrowded, prisons generally met international standards.

<u>Physical Conditions</u>: According to the Prisons and Parole Act, pretrial detainees should be held separately from convicted prisoners, but this was not always followed. The MCS oversaw the operation of three prison facilities: Maafushi Prison, Asseyri Prison, and Male Prison. The MCS also operated Hulhumale Detention Center and the Ahuluveri Marukazu rehabilitation center for upcoming parolees, while the MPS operated Dhoonidhoo pretrial Detention Center and Male Custodial Center. Detainees reported overcrowding and inadequate hygiene and sanitation standards in prisons and pretrial detention facilities. The MCS prison system, with an estimated capacity of 1,365 prisoners and detainees, had a prison population of 1,504 as of October. The MPS detention system, with an estimated capacity of 337 detainees, had a detainee population of 376 as of November. Local NGO Maldivian Democracy Network (MDN) claimed prisoners lacked access to adequate and timely medical services in Dhoonidhoo Detention Center, especially for arrested opposition protesters. The MDN reported prison officials selectively provided medical access to detainees. Some high-profile convicts reported being denied permission to travel abroad for necessary medical treatment. There were also reports authorities occasionally held migrant workers in a facility that also housed pretrial detainees. Three detainees died in MPS or MCS custody during the year. Both the HRCM and NIC were investigating the cases and were yet to report their findings.

<u>Administration</u>: A police procedure introduced March 20 prohibits meetings between detainees and legal counsel on Fridays and public holidays. Former solicitor general Ibrahim Riffath called the new procedure "unconstitutional," saying only a law passed by parliament could narrow fundamental rights or freedoms. The law was used in May to stop one detainee, who was arrested while protesting against the development of the China-Maldives Friendship Bridge, from meeting his lawyer.

<u>Independent Monitoring</u>: The government generally permitted regular and unannounced prison visits by the HRCM, which provided recommendations to the government to address deficiencies. As of August the HRCM conducted 11 visits to prisons and other government centers. The government generally permitted visits by the International Committee of the Red Cross/Red Crescent and other international assessment teams. The committee conducted visits to prisons and police stations in January.

d. Arbitrary Arrest or Detention

The law prohibits arbitrary arrest and detention; however, the government failed to enforce the law consistently, especially in cases against members of the political opposition.

Role of the Police and Security Apparatus

The MPS is responsible for internal security, public safety, and law and order, and is subordinate to the Ministry of Home Affairs. The Maldives National Defense Force (MNDF) is responsible for external security and disaster relief, but the MPS at times requested its assistance in matters of internal security and law and order during some political protests. The chief of the MNDF reports to the minister of defense. The president is commander in chief of the MNDF.

Civilian authorities generally maintained control over the MPS and MNDF, and the government had generally effective mechanisms to investigate and punish abuse and corruption. The NIC, formed in October 2015, replaced the Police Integrity Commission as the primary mechanism to investigate abuses by law enforcement agencies and employees, and it has the authority to forward any cases with criminal elements to police for further investigation. The NIC reported it received 84 complaints of MPS human rights violations as of July 31, but it had completed investigations in only one of the cases. Human rights organizations reported allegations of police brutality were not fairly adjudicated by the courts and, as a result, police enjoyed impunity.

There is no independent review mechanism to investigate abuses by military forces. Parliament and the judiciary, however, could initiate investigations on an ad hoc basis. There were no reported complaints of human rights abuses by military forces, and military operations generally remained separate from civilian political activities.

Arrest Procedures and Treatment of Detainees

The law states an arrest may not be made unless the arresting officer observes the offense, has reasonable evidence, or has a court-issued arrest warrant. According to the MPS, however, if a police officer has reason to believe that a person has committed, is committing, or is about to commit an offense, s/he may arrest the person. The constitution provides for an arrestee to be verbally informed immediately of the reason for arrest and to be informed in writing within 24 hours. Prisoners have the right to a ruling on bail within 36 hours, but bail procedures were not implemented consistently. The law also requires an arrestee be informed of the right to remain silent and have access a lawyer at the time of arrest. A lawyer may be court appointed in serious criminal cases if the accused cannot afford one. Authorities generally permitted detainees to have counsel present during police questioning. Police normally informed the arrestee's family of the arrest within 24 hours, although the law does not require that police inform the family of the grounds for the arrest.

The law provides for investigative detention. Once a person is detained, the arresting officer must present evidence to a court within 24 hours to justify continued detention. Based on the evidence presented, the prosecutor general has the authority to determine whether charges may be filed. If law enforcement authorities are unable to present sufficient evidence within 24 hours, the prisoner is eligible for release. Judges have the authority to extend detention at 15-day intervals upon receiving an arresting officer's petition, citing factors such as the detainee's previous criminal record, status of the investigation, type of offense in question, and whether the detainee posed a threat if released.

Arbitrary Arrest: The NIC confirmed proper arrest procedures were in place but noted police did not always fully implement them due to lack of adequate training. Sources reported police held suspects under investigative or administrative detention without formal arrest for periods ranging from a few hours to several weeks. Police allegedly used this procedure to remove opposition supporters and journalists from the streets, and to control gang activities.

In November 2015 social media activist Ahmed Ashraf was arrested in Sri Lanka and returned to Maldives. The Sri Lankan Department of Immigration and Emigration issued a statement stating it allowed Ashraf's repatriation based on a request received by the Maldivian High Commission in Colombo, but according to a November 2015 statement from the Sri Lankan Foreign Ministry, his repatriation may have violated Sri Lankan immigration laws. Ashraf was one of eight "suspects of terrorism" allegedly linked to the 2015 explosion of President Yameen's speedboat. During the year the PGO charged Ashraf for a separate crime, and he remained in remand.

<u>Detainee's Ability to Challenge Lawfulness of Detention before a Court</u>: The constitution stipulates conditions under which a person can be arrested or detained and provides everyone the right to appeal and the right to compensation for unlawful arrest or detention. Various laws and regulations govern arrest and detention procedures. The High Court routinely hears appeals of arrest warrants or pretrial detention orders, but defense lawyers claimed High Court judges tend to seek justification for upholding such orders rather than questioning the grounds and merits of detention. In October the PGO declined to press charges against Shamoon Jaleel, a social media activist who was held in pretrial detention for more than 40 days, citing lack of evidence. Jaleel had previously appealed his detention at the High Court, which had ruled to uphold the order. The appeal courts do not accept appeals of detentions authorized for the duration of an ongoing trial, based on a 2012 High Court decision that ruled trial judges have discretionary authority to authorize detention of suspects for the duration of ongoing trials and a 2009 Supreme Court decision that stated decisions made by judges using discretionary authority cannot be appealed. In March the High Court dismissed an appeal filed by a former magistrate judge using this justification.

Victims of unlawful or arbitrary arrest or detention can submit cases to the Civil Court to seek compensation but this right was not commonly exercised.

e. Denial of Fair Public Trial

The law provides for an independent judiciary, but the judiciary was not completely independent or impartial, and was subject to influence. There were numerous allegations of judicial impropriety and abuse of power. Government officials, opposition members, the UN High Commissioner for Human Rights, and members of domestic and international civil society at times accused the judiciary of bias and accused the executive branch of manipulating judicial outcomes. The Commonwealth Human Rights Initiative also alleged that the Supreme Court attempted to control the lower courts "to influence the administration of justice in the interest of the government." After her April 2015 visit, Mona Rishmawi, chief of the Rule of Law, Equality, and Non-Discrimination Branch at the Office of the High Commissioner for Human Rights stated the judicial system was perceived as politicized, inadequate, and subject to external influence. In their joint August 2015 report, the International Commission of Jurists and South Asians for Human

Rights (SAHR) alleged the government, in particular the ruling Progressive Party of Maldives (PPM), manipulated the judiciary to "further vested interests."

The five-member Supreme Court is constitutionally independent from the executive. It hears appeals from the High Court and considers constitutional matters brought directly before it. In June 2015 the Supreme Court issued an 11-point guideline barring the HRCM from communicating with foreign organizations without government oversight and cited the HRCM's submission to the Universal Periodic Review (UPR) as treasonous. In its 2015 annual report released in March, the HRCM stated the guideline was "the biggest challenge" to the commission's ability to do its work. On September 25, the International Service for Human Rights filed a case with the UN Human Rights Committee on behalf of two former HRCM commissioners alleging the guideline violated international law by restricting human rights defenders from submitting information to the United Nations. In response the HRCM released an October 7 statement defending the guideline by claiming it did not impede the HRCM's ability to cooperate with the United Nations, in direct contradiction to the guideline. Many judges, appointed for life, held only a certificate in sharia, not a law degree. Most magistrate judges could not interpret common law or sharia because they lacked adequate English or Arabic language skills. An estimated one-quarter of the country's 183 judges had criminal records. Media, human rights organizations, and NGOs criticized the Judicial Service Commission (JSC) for appointing unqualified judges and, according to a 2016 Commonwealth Human Rights Initiative report, the composition of the JSC, tasked with vetting and appointing judges, is flawed, leading to a politicized judiciary. In its report the Commonwealth Human Rights Initiative accused the Supreme Court of harshly targeting independent institutions and lawyers and failing to guarantee the right to a fair trial to accused. There was no government response.

In June the Supreme Court rejected former defense minister Colonel Mohamed Nazim's appeal of his March 2015 conviction on charges of importation and possession of illegal weapons. On June 21, just after Nazim filed the appeal but prior to the Supreme Court ruling, the MPS revealed the investigations into Nazim's case were incomplete, adding it uncovered new evidence not previously available to the court that may exonerate him. The Supreme Court did not consider this additional evidence when deciding on Nazim's appeal. During Nazim's trial, the High Court denied the defense team's request to present rebuttal evidence it claimed would have exonerated Nazim.

Trial Procedures

The law provides that an accused person is presumed innocent until proven guilty. Most trials were public and conducted by judges and magistrates, some of whom were trained in Islamic, civil, or criminal law. Regulations rather than laws govern trial procedures. Judges question the concerned parties and attempt to establish the facts of a case. Accused persons have the right to defend themselves and during a trial may call witnesses and retain the right to legal representation. Defendants and their attorneys have the right to full access to all evidence relating to their case, may cross-examine any witnesses presented by the state, and may present their own witnesses and evidence. The judiciary generally enforced these rights, with a few notable exceptions.

In the case of at least one death row convict, Hussain Humaam, MDN and other human rights advocates insisted due process rights were ignored. Humaam was accused of murdering parliamentarian Afrasheem Ali, who was found dead in October 2012. Humaam was 19 years old at the time of the incident. NGOs reported there were multiple contradictions in witness testimonies and evidence presented during the trial, making it impossible to arrive at a verdict "beyond any doubt", as required by law. The Criminal Court found Humaam guilty of murder in January 2013. In December 2015, the High Court upheld the verdict, and on June 24, the Supreme Court unanimously upheld the original conviction. With the Supreme Court's ruling, only an official pardon from the victim's family could get Humaam off death row.

Under existing death penalty provisions and in Islamic law, a case must be proven "beyond any doubt" to be eligible for a death penalty verdict. For cases where the death penalty is imposed for qisas (retaliation in kind under Maldives Islamic law), the heirs of the deceased must agree to the punishment. In the event the heirs are below the age of 18, Islamic law jurisprudence requires the state to halt the implementation of the death penalty until the children reach 18 and can give their agreement.

Islamic law as interpreted by the country is applied in situations not covered by civil law. The law provides for the right to legal counsel, and those convicted have the right to appeal. The testimony of women is equal to that of men in court, except on rape and other issues specifically stipulated by the country's legal code.

Political Prisoners and Detainees

The government asserted there were no political prisoners; however, the opposition, international and domestic NGOs, and members of the international community estimated there were at least two political prisoners and likely many more. Former president Mohamed Nasheed, who is leader of the opposition Maldivian Democratic Party (MDP) and ran against President Yameen during the 2013 presidential election, was subjected to a rushed trial and many of his due process rights were ignored, according to international observers. The UN Working Group on Arbitrary Detentions in September 2015 determined Nasheed's detention was politically motivated and opined there were serious due-process violations that indicated Nasheed had not received a free and fair trial. The government announced its rejection of the working group's findings in a September 2015 press release. In January the government granted approval for Nasheed to travel to London on a medical furlough. He remained in London at year's end and stated he was unable to return due to concerns he would again be arbitrarily detained.

Opposition Adhaalath Party leader Sheikh Imran was arrested in May 2015 on terrorism charges on the grounds his speech at an opposition rally incited protesters to become violent. Human rights NGO TM, however, asserted "during the speech Sheikh Imran repeatedly denied any intent of violence against the government." On February 16, a court sentenced Imran to 12 years' imprisonment.

Civil Judicial Procedures and Remedies

Individuals or organizations may seek civil remedies for human rights violations. The Civil Court addressed noncriminal cases.

f. Arbitrary or Unlawful Interference with Privacy, Family, Home, or Correspondence

The law prohibits security officials from opening or reading radio messages, letters, or telegrams, or monitoring telephone conversations, "except as expressly provided by law." Security forces may open the mail of private citizens and monitor telephone conversations if authorized to do so by a court during a criminal investigation. There were reports, nevertheless, of illegal recording of telephone conversations and monitoring of text messages allegedly executed by the MNDF and other government agencies.

Section 2. Respect for Civil Liberties, Including:

a. Freedom of Speech and Press

The constitution provides for freedom of speech and press, except on religious matters, but the government imposed legal restrictions on this freedom.

Freedom of Speech and Expression: The Antidefamation and Freedom of Expression Act enacted in August criminalizes any expression that "contradicts a tenet of Islam, threatens national security, contradicts social norms, or encroaches on another's rights, reputation, or good name." The bill imposes fines of up to two million Maldivian rufiyaa (MVR) ($129,700) for violations and jail terms of up to six months for failure to pay fines. A fine can only be appealed after it is paid. According to the law, journalists can also be required to reveal the sources of alleged defamatory statements in direct contravention to Article 28 of the constitution, which states, "No person should be compelled to disclose the source of any information that is espoused, disseminated, or published by that person." In August UN Special Rapporteur on Freedom of Expression David Kaye asserted the law limits the right to freedom of expression to such a degree that the right itself is in jeopardy. Political opposition parties and major NGOs condemned the bill as having an adverse effect on fundamental freedoms of expression.

Youth Ministry regulations prohibit publishing literary material without first seeking authorization from the National Bureau of Classification. The regulations define publication of literary material as "any writing, photograph, or drawing that has been made publicly accessible electronically or by way of printing, including publicizing or circulating on the internet."

On several occasions police sought to limit free speech and expression by arresting and questioning individuals who participated in opposition political protests. Journalists in particular were routinely detained while covering protests and held for several hours before being released without charges. According to media sources, the government directly and indirectly forbade civil servants from attending political protests, and some employees of public and private institutions were fired for similar reasons. Opposition parties reported difficulty conducting lawful rallies because of August amendments to the Freedom of Peaceful Assembly Act that imposed additional restrictions on planning and execution of protests. Police and members of the military routinely monitored opposition rallies.

The constitution prohibits utterances contrary to tenets of Islam or the government's religious policies.

<u>Press and Media Freedoms</u>: Independent media were active and expressed a wide variety of views. Criticism of the government and debates on societal problems were commonplace, but media did not question Islamic values or the government's policies on religion.

A number of government actions resulted in obstructions to independent media, including the passage of the Antidefamation and Freedom of Expression Act that compels journalists to reveal their sources in violation of the constitution. The act also imposes heavy fines against outlets that broadcast criminalized content and allows the government to revoke licenses of websites and outlets which fail to pay the fines. Journalists expressed concern most media outlets cannot afford the fines.

In March, following the Civil Court order to halt publication of the country's oldest daily newspaper, *Haveeru*, the newspaper's owners complied. Observers believed the government closed the newspaper because the government could not control its content or influence. In its final ruling on the case issued in July, the Civil Court barred former staff of *Haveeru* from working at any other media organization or media-related businesses until February 2018, after its reporters resigned en masse following the March shutdown to form a new newspaper, *Mihaaru*. Attorney General Mohamed Anil declared the court order unconstitutional and an obstruction of the right to work and filed an appeal of the order at the High Court.

In May 3, Raajje TV journalists were charged with obstruction of law enforcement officers after being arrested while covering an opposition protest and a bomb scare in 2015. A fourth journalist from the same outlet was also charged with assault for allegedly "touching" a police officer as he was arrested while covering a bomb scare in 2015. The Criminal Court hearings were taking place, but media claimed the charges were part of the government's systematic attempts to silence free speech.

<u>Violence and Harassment</u>: Authorities allegedly attacked, harassed, and intimidated media representatives.

On February 13, hours after Raajje TV announced a new program detailing corruption allegations against President Yameen, police entered the Raajje TV office without a court warrant to arrest a reporter for allegedly taking a photograph of a police operation. The journalist was released without charges hours later and filed complaints with the HRCM and the Maldives Broadcasting Commission. There was no indication either authority took steps to investigate the case.

In April police detained, but released hours later, 18 journalists protesting threats to press freedom. The female journalists were repeatedly strip searched in an area easily accessible to the entire station.

<u>Censorship or Content Restrictions</u>: The Parliament Privileges Act and the Antidefamation and Freedom of Expression Act allow authorities to force journalists to reveal their sources, but authorities did not routinely take advantage of this provision. Media reported higher levels of self-censorship in reporting political news following the passage of the Antidefamation and Freedom of Expression Act. Members of civil society and journalists said crackdowns on political opposition members led them to self-censor.

In August the Maldives Broadcasting Commission ordered Medianet, the only private cable television provider in the country, to be more careful about self-censorship to avoid broadcasting "content which breaches social norms." The commission claimed it received complaints of inappropriate content from some viewers. The order came one day after the ratification of the Antidefamation and Freedom of Expression Act.

NGO sources stated media practiced self-censorship on matters related to Islam due to fears of harassment from being labeled "anti-Islamic." Journalists also practiced self-censorship in reporting on problems in the judiciary or criticizing the judiciary.

There were no known restrictions on domestic publications, nor were there prohibitions on the import of foreign publications or materials, except for those containing pornography or material otherwise deemed objectionable to Islamic values, such as Bibles and idols for worship. The restriction applies only to items for public distribution; tourists destined for resort islands were not prohibited from carrying Bibles and other religious paraphernalia for their personal use.

Internet Freedom

The government generally did not restrict or disrupt access to the internet or censor online content, and there were no credible reports that the government monitored private online communications without appropriate legal authority. According to the International Telecommunication Union, an estimated 270,000 residents of the country (69 percent of the population) had reliable access to the internet as of June. The Communications Authority of Maldives (CAM) is the regulatory body mandated to enforce internet content restrictions on sites hosted within the country and to block domestic access to any websites. CAM maintained an unpublished blacklist of all offending websites. CAM reported it blocked one website in 2016, Addu Live, for ignoring mandatory registration requirements but stated the site was unblocked after the owner complied. CAM did not proactively monitor internet content; instead, it relied on requests from ministries and other government agencies to block websites that violate domestic laws on anti-Islamism, pornography, child abuse, sexual and domestic violence, and other prohibitions. The MPS reported it did not investigate any websites for unlawful content related to prohibitions on anti-Islamic rhetoric, pornography, child abuse, sexual and domestic violence, or other violations as of August.

Academic Freedom and Cultural Events

The law prohibits public statements contrary to the government's policy on religion or the government's interpretation of Islam. In response to the law, there were credible reports academics practiced self-censorship. The government censored course content and curricula. Sunni Islam was the only religion taught in schools.

b. Freedom of Peaceful Assembly and Association

Freedom of Assembly

The constitution provides for "freedom of peaceful assembly without prior permission of the State," but the government did not respect this. In 2013 the president signed a law on peaceful assembly that restricted protests outside designated areas, and in August the president ratified an amendment to the law further restricting the designated areas for lawful protests. Protesters must now obtain prior written permission from the MPS to hold protests in restricted areas in violation of the constitution. Opposition political parties expressed concern the amendment effectively banned protests in the city.

Freedom of Association

The constitution provides for freedom of association, but the government imposed some limits on this freedom. The government only allowed clubs and other private associations that did not contravene Islamic or civil law to register.

The Political Parties Act restricts registration of political parties and eligibility of state funds to those parties with 10,000 or more members. Existing parties with fewer than 10,000 members had three months to acquire enough members or they would be ineligible for state funding. On August 17, the president ratified an amendment to the act requiring all political parties to submit fingerprints with each membership application, legalizing a 2011 Elections Commission (EC) requirement. Forms without fingerprints would be considered invalid, and those persons would not be counted as members of a political party. TM and MDN raised concerns the law and subsequent amendments restricted the constitutional right to form and participate in political parties.

c. Freedom of Religion

See the Department of State's *International Religious Freedom Report* at www.state.gov/religiousfreedomreport/.

d. Freedom of Movement, Internally Displaced Persons, Protection of Refugees, and Stateless Persons

The law provides for freedom of internal movement, foreign travel, emigration, and repatriation, and the government generally respected these rights.

Exile: The new Penal Code abolishes the use of banishment to a remote island as a punishment. Such sentences were common in the past. The implementation of such punishment was difficult, however, because host communities increasingly refused to accept anyone sentenced for a crime. According to MCS statistics, there were nine individuals serving banishment sentences for periods shorter than life.

Emigration and Repatriation: Maldives Immigration reported its Expatriate Monitoring and Repatriation Section had an active voluntary repatriation system, and between January and August, 2,403 foreigners, mostly from Bangladesh, voluntarily repatriated to their home countries. In an August tweet, Maldives Immigration stated a further 2,597 foreign resident workers had been repatriated for irregularities with their documentation, including 230 who were deported. Foreign workers may initiate voluntary repatriation proceedings, but Maldives Immigration interviews employers to recover withheld passports, request payment of return airfare for the foreign worker if applicable, and identify whether the foreign worker had abandoned his or her duties without proper notice.

<u>Citizenship</u>: The law requires all citizens to be Sunni Muslims.

Protection of Refugees

<u>Access to Asylum</u>: The law does not provide for the granting of asylum or refugee status, and the government has not established a system for providing protection to refugees.

Section 3. Freedom to Participate in the Political Process

The constitution provides citizens the ability to choose their government in free and fair periodic elections held by secret ballot and based on universal and equal suffrage.

Elections and Political Participation

<u>Recent Elections</u>: The parliamentary elections held in March 2014 were well administered and transparent, according to TM, "but wider issues of money politics threatens to hijack [the] democratic process." TM also concluded the 2013 presidential elections "were credible, transparent and extremely well administered" with "unprecedented voter turnout," but TM revealed a survey conducted prior to the 2013 presidential election showed 15 percent of respondents were offered "money or other incentives" in exchange for their vote. TM reported vote buying was even more widespread in the subsequent parliamentary elections due to gaps in the electoral legal framework, lack of coordination, and a failure to take action by the relevant institutions.

<u>Political Parties and Political Participation</u>: An August amendment to the Political Parties Act requires all parties to obtain fingerprints from all their members. The law enshrines a 2011 EC regulation that came into effect years after most of the country's political parties were established, except for the president's PPM. The size of a party's membership is tied to the amount of state funding it can receive. In October the EC officially amended the membership numbers of all political parties based on compliance with the biometric regulation, and all parties, except the ruling PPM, saw a decline in membership.

In 2015 President Yameen ratified an amendment to the Prisons and Parole Act prohibiting inmates from holding senior or leadership positions in political parties, effectively stripping former president Nasheed of the MDP presidency. As a result of a split in the president's PPM between President Yameen and political rival former president Maumoon, Yameen's supporters twice vandalized a PPM office being used by Maumoon's supporters. The first incident occurred October 30 where the MPS assisted Yameen's supporters to break the lock and enter the building. The second incident occurred on November 3 where Yameen's supporters smeared oil around the office. Opposition supporters publicly asserted these incidents were yet another example of presidential impunity.

The judiciary also asserted its ability to interfere in the administration of political parties. On October 16, the Civil Court issued an order handing control over the administration of the PPM temporarily to President Yameen, despite former president Maumoon's official chairmanship of the party. Both the High Court and the Supreme Court upheld this court order.

Participation of Women and Minorities: Women were traditionally active in public life, but a February release from SAHR indicated female parliamentarians were publicly assaulted in parliament and were threatened with rape by male parliamentarians. On February 24, a male parliamentarian spit on a female parliamentarian during parliamentary debate, leading SAHR to condemn the speaker of parliament's failure to reprimand the offending parliamentarian as a de facto endorsement of the humiliation of female parliamentarians. There were five women in the 85-member parliament.

Section 4. Corruption and Lack of Transparency in Government

The law provides criminal penalties for corruption by officials, but the government did not implement the law effectively, and officials frequently engaged in corrupt practices with impunity.

Corruption: The independent Anticorruption Commission (ACC) has responsibility for investigating corruption charges involving senior government officials. According to the commission, a limited definition of corruption in the law and the lack of a provision to investigate and prosecute illicit enrichment limited the commission's work. The Commonwealth Human Rights Initiative, which conducted a November 2015 fact-finding mission, concluded independent institutions like the ACC were unable to fulfil their mandate due to "incessant interference from the judiciary and the government." As of July, the ACC received 395 registered cases.

NGOs noted there was an increase in corruption practices at all levels of society, and the ACC reported it received one registered case of a company belonging to ruling-party members or parliamentarians winning a disproportionate number of bids. Judges were commonly believed to take bribes, and the ACC reported it was looking into one such case. The president and ruling-party members of parliament were widely accused of illicit enrichment. Vote buying in parliament reportedly affected key constitutional amendments and other legislation.

TM reported widespread corruption across the judiciary, legislature, and the executive branches and, in a September 9 statement, called on "all state institutions to address allegations of widespread corruption and conduct an independent investigation free from political influence." TM also expressed concern in a June 30 statement about "the increasing intimidation and challenges faced by watchdog bodies, activists, and media outlets reporting on corruption."

Al Jazeera released a documentary on September 7 focused on corruption in President Yameen's administration. The documentary alleged widespread corruption in the leasing of local islands, judicial bribery, state-sponsored violence against media, and hinted at the existence of an international network to launder money through the Maldives Monetary Authority. The documentary asserted President Yameen personally received millions of dollars from illegal island leasing. TM and several political opposition members called for an independent investigation into the allegations.

Financial Disclosure: The constitution requires members of parliament to submit annually to the secretary general of parliament a statement of all property owned, money, business interests, and liabilities. The constitution also requires the president and each cabinet minister to submit a similar statement to the auditor general, and for each judge to submit a similar statement to the JSC. It was unclear whether officials submitted these statements, which do not require public disclosure. In November TM told media it submitted a request under the Right to Information (RTI) Act seeking a list of all parliamentarians who declared their assets as required by law but the Speaker of parliament rejected the request. The law does not stipulate criminal or administrative sanctions for noncompliance and does not require the vice president to disclose income and assets.

Public Access to Information: Under the RTI Act the public has access to government information. The Office of the Information Commissioner received 21 requests under this law as of August. No data were available on the number of RTI requests submitted to other government offices.

Section 5. Governmental Attitude Regarding International and Nongovernmental Investigation of Alleged Violations of Human Rights

A number of domestic and international human rights groups generally operated without government restriction, investigating and publishing their findings on human rights cases. Government officials rarely were cooperative and responsive to their views. TM and other NGOs reported an associations regulation passed October 2015 threatened their freedom of operation. The regulation requires human rights and other NGOs to seek government approval before applying for domestic assistance above 25,000 MVR ($1,630) and for any foreign assistance. The regulation also requires organizations to submit a membership registry to the government, and grants the registrar of associations sweeping powers to dissolve organizations and enter organizations to obtain documents without a search warrant.

The United Nations or Other International Bodies: Following a decision by the Commonwealth Ministerial Action Group to place a review of the human rights situation in the country on its formal agenda, President Yameen announced in October the country would withdraw from the Commonwealth.

Government Human Rights Bodies: The HRCM is a constitutionally recognized independent institution with a mandate to promote and protect human rights under the constitution, Maldivian Islamic law, and regional and international human rights conventions ratified by the country.

In 2014 the Supreme Court summoned all members of the HRCM to condemn the critical statements it made regarding the court in a UPR submission to the UN Human Rights Council (UNHRC); thereafter the HRCM was relatively inactive. In June 2015 the Supreme Court issued a judgment that the HRCM's submission to the UPR was unlawful, biased, and undermined judicial independence. The government replaced the HRCM's five members in August 2015 after the commissioners' term limits expired. Opposition political parties criticized the appointments, alleging the new members were close allies of President Yameen and the ruling PPM government. The Commonwealth Human Rights Initiative claimed in its 2016 report, *Searching for a Lost Democracy*, that these "arbitrary dismissals and pro-ruling party appointments" affected the HRCM's ability to fulfil its mandate.

In a September 2015 public writ, the Supreme Court ordered the Attorney General's Office to represent all state offices, including independent institutions, in "proceedings where offices and institutions of the state have submitted a claim, and where charges have been filed against them." Many NGOs criticized the writ as compromising the independence of the HRCM because it contravened the Human Rights Commission Act, and the acts of other independent institutions, which state that these commissions are "separate legal entities" with the authority "to sue and suit against, and to make undertakings in its own capacity."

Section 6. Discrimination, Societal Abuses, and Trafficking in Persons

Women

Rape and Domestic Violence: Laws that came into effect in 2014 regarding sexual harassment and sexual offenses criminalize spousal rape and gender discrimination in workplaces, including in educational institutions and service providers such as hospitals. A man may be convicted of rape in the absence of a confession only if there are two male witnesses or four female witnesses willing to testify. In the case of a child, the burden of proof is lower.

As of October 31, the MPS received seven reports of rape, one of which it had forwarded for prosecution. It also received 262 reports of various sexual offenses and forwarded 44 of these to the PGO. Eight of these cases led to prosecution and charges.

Media reports of violence against women and rape were common. Most rape and abuse cases reported in media involved minors, and attackers usually knew their victims. NGOs believed many more cases remained unreported due to fear of reprisals, losing custody of children, lack of economic independence, insensitivity of police in dealing with victims, absence of regulation in media concerning victims' privacy, the stigma of being a victim, and low conviction rates.

As of October 31, 553 cases of domestic violence were reported to the MPS. The MPS forwarded 30 of these cases to the PGO for prosecution, one of which led to a conviction. The law covering all types of domestic relations prohibits physical, sexual, verbal, psychological, and financial abuse. It also extends protection to wives against being forcibly impregnated by their husbands against medical orders and includes an extensive list of other abuses for which protection is provided. The act allows courts to issue restraining orders in domestic violence cases and criminalizes any actions against these orders. Officers were nevertheless reluctant to make arrests in cases of violence against women within the family, reportedly believing such violence was justified. A World Bank report, *Understanding*

Gender in Maldives, found that, despite the passage of the domestic violence legislation, a majority of women named gender-based violence as one of their major concerns.

Female Genital Mutilation/Cutting (FGM/C): There were no data on the frequency of FGM/C, although religious leaders called for the practice to be revived in 2014. Local NGO Hope for Women reported the practice persisted, but societal stigma restricted public discussion of the issue.

Other Harmful Traditional Practices: In September 2015 the president ratified the third amendment to the Penal Code, which stated only Maldivian Islamic law penalties may be imposed for hadd (robbery, fornication, homosexual acts, alcohol consumption, apostasy) and qisas (retaliation in kind) offenses. Penalties could include hand amputation for theft and stoning to death for adultery. In October 2015 the Supreme Court annulled a death by stoning verdict of one woman. Prior to the amendment, the Penal Code only allowed for the implementation of milder penalties in limited cases, including flogging for fornication and optional flogging for consuming alcohol and pork, not fasting during Ramadan, and for perjury.

In its February 2015 submission to the second UPR on the country, Amnesty International called for a moratorium on flogging as a form of punishment. In the government's response to the UPR in May 2015, the secretary of legal affairs defended the practice of flogging, stating, "Maldivians believe that Islamic principles and human rights go hand in hand" and that flogging is a useful crime deterrent.

Sexual Harassment: The law bans sexual harassment in the workplace, but the government did not enforce the law. There were allegations of sexual harassment in government ministries and the private sector.

The MPS reported 19 filed cases of sexual harassment from January to October 31 under the Sexual Harassment Act, one of which it forwarded for prosecution.

To streamline the process of reporting abuse against women and children, there were family and children's centers on every atoll. According to the HRCM, these centers also provided services for neglected children, support for families unable to take of their children, and women with mental or other disabilities. The Ministry of Gender and Family reported the need to establish residential facilities at family and children's centers on every atoll to provide emergency shelter assistance to domestic violence and other victims, but these were yet to be established.

<u>Reproductive Rights</u>: Married couples by law have the right to decide the number, spacing, and timing of their children; manage their reproductive health; and have access to the information and means to do so, free from coercion, or violence. There were some reports of employment discrimination based on a woman's perceived reproductive plans. Unmarried couples and single women did not have the legal right to access contraception but could obtain contraception over the counter on larger islands. Access to information on contraception and skilled attendants at delivery and in postpartum care were widely available on larger islands but more difficult to find on smaller, more remote islands. According to UN Population Fund (UNFPA) statistics released in October, the country's maternal mortality rate declined 90 percent in the last 25 years, with only 68 women dying out of every 100,000 live births in 2015 when compared with 677 deaths out of every 100,000 live births in 1990. UNFPA attributed this improvement to developments in the country's health and emergency obstetric care, as well as to increased public awareness about the importance of prenatal care.

<u>Discrimination</u>: Discrimination against women remained a problem. Authorities more readily accused women of adultery, in part because visible pregnancies made the allegedly adulterous act more obvious, while men could deny the charges and escape punishment because of the difficulty of proving fornication or adultery under Islamic law.

Under Islamic practice, husbands may divorce their wives more easily than wives may divorce their husbands. Islamic law also governs estate inheritance, which grants male heirs twice the share of female heirs. According to the PGO, however, property was generally divided equally among siblings unless the men in the family demanded a larger share.

In March the government adopted the National Gender Equality Policy, and on August 23, parliament passed a Gender Equality Law, to become effective in February 2017. According to the HRCM, however, there were no policies in place to provide equal opportunities for women's employment, despite provisions in the constitution and the law. According to a World Bank report, *Understanding Gender in Maldives*, women tended to be clustered in low-growth sectors and lower-paying positions than men and tended to earn less than men for equal work. The absence of child-care facilities made it difficult for women to remain employed after they had children and social stigma about some industries and jobs limited women's job opportunities. Societal disapproval also discouraged women from working at tourist resorts for extended periods. According to the World Bank report *Women, Business, and the Law*, employers can legally ask employees about their marital status and reproductive plans, leading to reports received by the HRCM that some employers discouraged women from marriage or pregnancy, since it could result in termination or demotion. The HRCM reported the government fell short of promoting women's equality by failing to establish childcare centers and child-friendly working environments, and failing to implement affirmative action.

Although women historically played a subordinate role in society, they participated in public life. Women accounted for 55 percent of civil service employees and 34 percent of the senior jobs as of July 31.

Children

Birth Registration: Citizenship is derived through one's parents. A child born of a citizen father or mother, regardless of the child's place of birth, may derive citizenship.

Education: Girls' access to secondary education was sometimes limited because of a lack of access to sanitation and separate facilities to study. NGO sources stated there were increasing reports of families preventing girls from going to school. According to NGO sources, school curricula reflected an increasingly "restrictive" interpretation of Islam.

Child Abuse: The Ministry of Gender and Family is in charge of following up on reports of child abuse, including cases of sexual abuse. The law stipulates sentences of up to 25 years in prison for those convicted of sexual offenses against children. If a person is legally married to a minor under Islamic law, however, none of the offenses specified in the legislation is considered crimes. The courts have the power to detain perpetrators, although most were released pending sentencing and allowed to return to the communities of their victims. In 2015 the Ministry of Gender and Family first published the online child sex offenders' registry that, as of September 18, listed 77 individuals and their photos, full names, identification card numbers, addresses, dates of conviction, dates of imprisonment, dates of scheduled release, and current whereabouts.

Reports of child abuse were on the rise, according to a 2015 release from the local NGO Advocating the Rights of Children (ARC). The organization noted existing cultural norms were creating a high-risk environment for children and called on the government to enact and enforce all the policies under the Child Rights Bill. In May 2015 the UN Children's Fund (UNICEF) launched an abuse-prevention program to increase awareness of child abuse, and in support of UNICEF's program, the Ministry of Gender and Family set up a child abuse reporting hotline where all calls were investigated and reported to police.

The Ministry of Gender and Family stated reports of sexual abuse were increasing, and underage marriage was a major concern. The increase in reported cases of sexual abuse appeared to result from increased public awareness, although the ministry noted there was still hesitation to report abuse occurring within the family.

Early and Forced Marriage: According to a September amendment to the Family Regulation, the Family Court must petition the Supreme Court for approval for girls and boys under age 18 to marry. The Ministry of Gender and Family must also submit an assessment of the proposed marriage to the Supreme Court and the marriage can only proceed after the Supreme Court grants the Family Court approval for the union. Three cases of underage marriage were reported to the Ministry of Gender and Family as of August, but the Department of Judicial Administration reported an increase in the number of cases where authorities failed to check the birth certificates of the underage bride and groom before they officiated the marriage. According to the NGO Hope for Women, Islamic scholars invited to speak at government-organized public events and on television and radio often endorsed early and forced marriage.

Female Genital Mutilation/Cutting (FGM/C): See women's section above.

Sexual Exploitation of Children: The Child Sexual Abuse (Special Provisions) Act prohibits child prostitution and the use, procurement, or provision of a child (below age 18) for the production of pornography or for pornographic performance. The crime is punishable by imprisonment between 15 and 25 years. The act stipulates that a child between ages 13 and 18 involved in a sexual act is deemed not to have given consent, "unless otherwise proven." The law also treats the prostitution of children by a third party as a form of human trafficking with exploitation under the Prevention of Human Trafficking Act with a 15-year maximum sentence. The law, however, generally requires the acts of exploitation be predicated on movement and does not criminalize it in the absence of coercion. The new Penal Code came into effect in July 2015 allowing the PGO to lodge multiple charges against a perpetrator for a single offense. For sex trafficking, this means the PGO can file charges for human trafficking under the Prevention of Human Trafficking Act and for prostitution under the Child Sexual Abuse Act, and aggregate the penalties so perpetrators serve longer sentences for a single offense.

<u>Institutionalized Children</u>: Local NGO ARC released a report in March detailing abuses in government-run "safe homes." These facilities were intended to be temporary stopovers for children being taken into state care, but ARC reported children routinely spent many months at these homes. According to ARC, the "safe homes" were inadequately furnished and equipped, lacked basic essentials, and were often understaffed, resulting in inadequate care, protection, and education for institutionalized children. Reiterating the findings from the UN Committee on the Rights of the Child's January report on Maldives, ARC also expressed concern about children living in the same living quarters as adults with serious mental disabilities in the government-run Home for People with Special Needs. The Ministry of Gender and Family reported it housed 163 children in its Kudakudhinge Hiya and Fiyavathi facilities. Police and the HRCM were investigating the October death of a five-month-old baby who was living at the Fiyavathi home but had not yet published their findings.

<u>International Child Abductions</u>: The country is not a party to the 1980 Hague Convention on the Civil Aspects of International Child Abduction. See the Department of State's *Annual Report on International Parental Child Abduction* at travel.state.gov/content/childabduction/en/legal/compliance.html.

Anti-Semitism

By law citizens may not practice any religion other than Sunni Islam; there were no Jewish residents. There were no reports of anti-Semitic acts.

Trafficking in Persons

See the Department of State's *Trafficking in Persons Report* at www.state.gov/j/tip/rls/tiprpt/.

Persons with Disabilities

The constitution and law provide for the rights and freedom from discrimination of persons with disabilities. The Disabilities Act provides for the protection of the rights of persons with disabilities, and financial assistance. Since the establishment of the National Registry of People with Disabilities in 2011, 6,417 persons had been registered as of August. The Act mandates the state to provide a monthly financial benefit of not less than 2,000 MVR ($130) to each registered individual.

Government services for persons with disabilities included special educational programs for those with sensory disabilities. Inadequate facilities and logistical challenges related to transporting persons with disabilities between islands and atolls made it difficult for persons with disabilities to participate in the workforce or consistently attend school.

Multiple NGOs worked to increase awareness and improve support for persons with disabilities. The Child Advocacy Network of Disability Organizations, established by ARC, launched a website in December 2015 containing detailed information on common types of disabilities in Maldives, and the services available for persons with disabilities from government authorities and NGOs.

The government integrated students with physical disabilities into mainstream educational programs. Children with disabilities had virtually no access or transition to secondary education. One mental health clinic in Male and several private health clinics employ psychiatrists and psychologists. They focused on a broad range of issues but service availability remained limited. There also was a lack of quality residential care.

Families usually cared for persons with disabilities. When family care was unavailable, adult individuals with disabilities lived in the Health Ministry's Home for People with Special Needs, which, as of July, housed 175 persons, 21 of whom were new placements during the year. The home accepted elderly persons and children as well. The government also provided assistance devices, such as wheelchairs, crutches, spectacles, hearing aids, and adapted seats for children with cerebral palsy.

Acts of Violence, Discrimination, and Other Abuses Based on Sexual Orientation and Gender Identity

The law prohibits same-sex sexual conduct. Under the new Penal Code, the punishment includes imprisonment of up to eight years, as well as a provision for a supplementary punishment of 100 lashes imposed under Maldives Islamic law. No organizations focused on lesbian, gay, bisexual, transgender, and intersex (LGBTI) problems in the country. There were no reports of officials complicit in abuses against LGBTI persons, although societal stigma likely discouraged individuals from reporting such problems. Due to societal intolerance of same-sex sexual relationships, there were few openly LGBTI individuals in the country, and no information was available on official or societal discrimination based on sexual orientation in employment, housing, access to education, or health care. NGOs reported several members of the LGBTI community sought refuge in Sri Lanka after societal shaming related to their sexual orientation.

Section 7. Worker Rights

a. Freedom of Association and the Right to Collective Bargaining

While the constitution provides for workers' freedom of association, there is no law protecting it, which is required to allow unions to register and operate without interference and discrimination. Worker organizations are treated as civil society organizations without the right to engage in collective bargaining. Police and armed forces do not have the right to form unions. The Freedom of Peaceful Assembly Act effectively prohibits strikes by workers in the resort sector, the country's largest money earner. Employees in the following services are also prohibited from striking: hospitals and health centers, electricity companies, water providers, telecommunications providers, prison guards, and air traffic controllers. The Home Ministry enforces the act by arresting workers who go on strike. There were widespread reports from civil society organizations that civil service employees were also discouraged from going on strikes or participating in political protests. The government threatened expulsion of migrant workers who participate in peaceful labor protests.

The government did not always enforce applicable laws. Resources, inspections, and remediation were inadequate, and penalties were not sufficient to deter violations. The government moved the Labor Relations Authority (LRA) to the Ministry of Economic Development in 2014. The LRA is mandated to oversee compliance of the Employment Act and its related regulations. The Employment Tribunal examines and adjudicates legal matters arising between employers and employees and other employment problems. The Employment Tribunal process is cumbersome and complicated. Violators who refused to correct violations or pay fines were referred to the courts, whose decisions often were ignored. The cases are heard in the Dhivehi language, which few foreign workers understand. Foreign workers may not file a case with the tribunal unless they appoint a representative to communicate for them in the local language. As of August the Employment Tribunal received 148 claims, 81 of which dealt with unfair dismissal. Most of the claims were for layoffs, contractual changes, and drug-related allegations or other criminal offenses.

Some workers' organizations were established under the law as civil society organizations, specifically in the tourism, education, health, and shipping (seafarers') sectors, although these functioned more as cooperative associations and had very limited roles in labor advocacy. The Teachers Association of the Maldives and the Tourism Employees Association of the Maldives (TEAM) were among the more active workers' organizations, along with the Maldives Fisherman's Association and Maldivian Ports Workers.

b. Prohibition of Forced or Compulsory Labor

All forms of forced or compulsory labor are prohibited, but the government did not effectively enforce applicable laws, and there were reports that forced labor occurred. Nevertheless, the LRA reported that officers were adequately trained to identify cases of forced labor and stated that the Prevention of Human Trafficking Act provided an effective solution.

Resources, inspections, and remediation were generally inadequate, and penalties were not sufficient to deter violations. The foreign worker population was particularly vulnerable to forced labor. Maldives Immigration detained undocumented workers at Hulhumale Detention Centre, an immigration-processing center near Male, until deportation or repatriation. There were reports of bureaucratic delays in processing undocumented immigrants and substandard facilities at the immigration-processing center. Maldives Immigration reported it screened the workers for victims of trafficking, but there were reports that some of the detained and deported undocumented workers should have been identified as trafficking victims.

Under the Penal Code, forced labor carries a penalty of up to eight years' imprisonment. Under Section 29 of the Maldives Prevention of Human Trafficking Act, confiscation, alteration, or withholding of identity and travel documents is a crime and perpetrators are subjected to up to five years' imprisonment, if found guilty. In April 2015 parliament approved the National Action Plan to Combat Trafficking in Persons for 2015-19. The penalty for human trafficking is a maximum sentence of 10 years. The PGO confirmed it did not prosecute any labor recruiters or agencies engaged in fraudulent practices during the year.

The LRA, under the Ministry of Economic Development, blacklisted companies that violated the law, precluding the companies from bringing in new workers until violations were rectified. Maldives Immigration enforced the blacklist, and blacklisted additional companies, although some companies resurfaced under different names. The law allows a fine of not more than 5,000 MVR ($325) for forced labor and other violations of the Employment Act. The government took steps to improve the conditions of migrant workers through the periodic distribution of pamphlets explaining their rights that were translated into languages commonly used by these workers.

As of August the government's Immigration Office reported the number of legal foreign workers at approximately 110,000. The Immigration Office estimated there were an additional 15,000-20,000 undocumented foreign workers in the country, mostly from Bangladesh and other South Asian countries. Some of these undocumented workers were subject to forced labor in the construction and tourism sectors. Most victims of forced labor suffered the following practices: debt bondage, holding of passports by employers, fraudulent offers of employment, not being paid the promised salary, or not being paid at all. Domestic workers, especially migrant female domestic workers, were sometimes trapped in forced servitude, in which employers used threats, intimidation, and in some cases sexual violence to prevent them from leaving.

Also, see the Department of State's *Trafficking in Persons Report* at www.state.gov/j/tip/rls/tiprpt/.

c. Prohibition of Child Labor and Minimum Age for Employment

The law sets the minimum age for employment at 16 years of age, with an exception for children who voluntarily participate in family businesses. The law prohibits employment of children under age 18 in "any work that may have a detrimental effect on health, education, safety, or conduct," but there was no list of such activities. As of August 10, the Civil Service Commission reported there were four civil servants between the ages of 16 and 18 working for the government.

The Ministry of Gender and Family; the Ministry of Economic Development; and the Family and Child Protection Unit of the MPS are tasked with receiving, investigating, and taking action on complaints of child labor. According to the LRA and the Ministry of Gender and Family, none of the complaints received related to child labor or employment of minors. Additionally, the LRA found no cases of child labor during its regular labor inspections during the year, nor were any cases of child labor reported to the ministry or to the HRCM. Resources, inspections, and remediation were inadequate, because no additional resources were dedicated specifically to uncover additional child labor cases.

The UNHRC expressed concerns that lack of data on children in the country engaged in the worst forms of child labor could lead to denial of a problem. The UNHRC was particularly concerned about children found in commercial sexual exploitation and girls working as domestics in private households.

Also, see the Department of Labor's *Findings on the Worst Forms of Child Labor* at dol.gov/ilab/reports/child-labor/findings/.

d. Discrimination with Respect to Employment and Occupation

The law and regulations prohibit discrimination with respect to employment and occupation on the basis of race, color, sex, political opinion, religion, national origin or citizenship, social origin, disability, language, age, sexual orientation or gender identity, and HIV-positive status or other communicable diseases. The government effectively enforced those laws and regulations, with some exceptions.

According to an HRCM report published in 2009, there were no policies in place to provide equal opportunities for women's employment, despite provisions in the constitution and the law. The law and constitution prohibit discrimination against women for employment or for equal pay or equal income, but in practice, women tended to earn less than men did because they tended to work in lower-paying industries. The absence of childcare facilities made it difficult for women with children to remain employed after they had children.

The Employment Act establishes an Employment Tribunal to examine and protect the rights of employers and employees in legal matters and other employment problems. In June President Yameen overhauled the seven-person tribunal by dismissing its president and vice president; he appointed two new members in July. According to the Employment Act, tribunal members can only be removed in cases of bankruptcy, incapacity, conviction, negligence, or contravening the oath of office. Civil society organizations asserted the former president and vice president did not violate any of these stipulations, and the surprise dismissal of the tribunal members led to allegations of executive branch control over tribunal decisions. Worker organization TEAM Secretary General Mauroof Zakir claimed President Yameen was misusing his authority to influence the tribunal's decisions, especially in cases in which someone was fired for exercising their constitutionally guaranteed right to freedom of assembly.

Discrimination against migrant workers was pervasive (see section 7. b.).

e. Acceptable Conditions of Work

The country does not have a national policy on minimum wage, and setting one would require an amendment to the Employment Act. Wages in the private sector were commonly set by contract between employers and employees and were based on rates for similar work in the public sector. The salary of the lowest-paid employee in the government sector was 3,100 MVR ($202) per month. According to TEAM, the average monthly salary for a worker employed on a tourism resort was 3,835 MVR ($250). According to 2016 Asian Development Bank statistics, 15 percent of Maldivians live below the poverty level of 29 MVR ($1.90) per day.

The law establishes maximum hours of work, overtime, annual and sick leave, maternity leave, and guidelines for workplace safety. The law provides for a 48-hour per week limit on work with a compulsory 24-hour break if employees work six days consecutively. Certain provisions in the law, such as overtime and public-holiday pay, do not apply to emergency workers, air and sea crews, executive staff of any company, or workers who are on call. The law mandates implementation of a safe workplace, procurement of secure tools and machinery, verification of equipment safety, use of protective equipment to mitigate health hazards, employee training in the use of protective gear, and appropriate medical care. All employers are required to provide health insurance for foreign workers.

There were no national standards for safety measures, and as a result, such measures were at the discretion of employers. In 2013 parliament approved the country's accession to eight core International Labor Organization conventions, but the government was yet to finalize the bills required for the conventions to be legislated into domestic law.

The LRA and Employment Tribunal are charged with implementing employment law and the LRA conducted workplace investigations and provided dispute resolution mechanisms to address complaints from workers. As of August 31, authorities completed inspections. The most common findings related to employment contracts and job descriptions, overtime and other pay, and problems related to leave. The LRA preferred to issue notices to employers to correct problems, because cases were deemed closed once fines were paid. The LRA typically gave employers one to three months to correct problems but lacked the resources to monitor compliance systematically. As of August 31, the LRA recommended seven companies for blacklisting through Maldives Immigration but did not fine any companies for noncompliance. According to Maldives Immigration, as of August there were 1,128 companies blacklisted over multiple years.

The LRA reported 102 labor-related complaints, 64 of which came from foreign workers.

Migrant workers were particularly vulnerable to exploitation, worked in unacceptable conditions, and were frequently forced to accept low wages to repay their debts with employment agencies. Employers often housed foreign workers at their worksites. Some migrant workers were exposed to dangerous working conditions, especially in the construction industry, and worked in hazardous environments without proper ventilation.

The Employment Act protects workers who remove themselves from situations that endanger health or safety without jeopardy to their employment, and authorities effectively protected employees in such situations.

www.ingramcontent.com/pod-product-compliance
Lightning Source LLC
Chambersburg PA
CBHW080819280726
48660CB00018B/3537